A STRANGER
IN SAN FRANCISCO
A poem in nine parts

Nick Freeth

Baffin Books

Published by Baffin Books UK, London

ISBN 978-1-9998198-6-6

Much of what I describe in this poem took place on my most recent visit to San Francisco, in October 2019. The concluding section, which refers to the coronavirus pandemic, was written in mid-2020.

Part IV features my versification of extracts from a log kept by a ship's carpenter, George William Mansfield, during his voyage aboard the barque *Lady Heathcote* from Liverpool to San Francisco and back in 1868-9. Its manuscript is in the permanent collection of the National Maritime Museum, Greenwich, London (Caird Library finding reference JOD/259/1), and I am grateful to the Museum for permission to use it. I have been unable to trace the copyright holder of a typewritten transcript of the log in the library (finding reference JOD/259/2), and any copyright infringement is unintentional.

I

I *Gotta Get Out of This Place*
And I've borrowed the Animals' line
Even though, unlike them, I just need a vacation.
Their song title may be a cliché that's set to three chords,
But it's more than the sum of its parts;
The stirrings it starts in listeners' thoughts
Could reset their bearings
And send them away
On a different course

My mind's ear will make the decision
When I'm choosing where I might be bound.
For me, it's a place's sound –
    the music, the murmuring landscapes
    and clamouring streets –
That all other pleasures
Coalesce around.

Aged about sixteen, I started listening
To bands from California;
Some records from L.A., but more from San Francisco.
I remember when I first put on the *Workingman's* LP
And heard a sweet guitar line
Cut through the noisy vinyl
Like sun across the City's foggy bay I'd never seen

The Grateful Dead, who made that album,
Had a seedy, tattered look
In the sepia-tinted photo on the cover
And the flip side of the High Time in their music
Was uncertainty and pain
As they sang about a dire wolf, a deadly speedway,
And a driver on cocaine

I liked the record's imperfections;
The voices were unpolished
But their characters and musical intentions
Were laid bare in their strivings:
Jerry's gentle touch with Robert Hunter's lyrics;
Weir's straight-ahead delivery;
And Pigpen's darker style of singing –
He inhabited the words
In a reckless, headlong way
Ignoring the warnings
Behind him and before him
He died aged twenty-seven in 1973.

I'm sometimes overwhelmed
By music's strange recesses
The points within its textures
Where harmonies emerge
From unfathomable places...
Like the moment in the sequence
On Side Two of *Live in Europe '72*

The first of the two numbers
Is by Hunter and Garcia,
And it leads into an instrumental section
Whose subtle interaction
Is driven by the bass and the guitars
And then, a mood of calm
Before those unexpected voices
Reach across the stillness
From infinitely far
  I know you rider...
  Lay down last night, I could not take my rest
  My mind was wand'ring...
  I wish I was a headlight on a train
  I'd shine my lamp
  To try and make a pathway through the rain
  I know you rider...

The very last refrain from that old song
Sung a cappella
    ...Going to miss me when I'm gone

Absences and distances
Far wider than the stereo
Highways and railroads
Sea to shining sea
Journeys much longer than any here in Britain
Where our little motorways and A- and B-roads
Can't measure up against the USA

But the Airplane and the Dead
And other lures and sirens
Haven't always been enough
To drag my ass across the ocean
In the face of the excuses I can find
To sit around at home
Instead of making up my mind to go...
Till finally, last summer,
I took a walk, to challenge my inertia,
Along the Great West Road and the A4
From Osterley to Heathrow...

II

...Where it's lunchtime on a Sunday –
Congregations
Are emerging from the churches
Placards
Berate the less-than-pious
    What do ye think of Jesus?;
    And the words from the Reproaches:
    O my people,
    What have I done to thee?
    Or wherein have I wearied thee?
    Answer me.

Around here there's no shortage
Of temptations and enticements
For travellers coming in and out of London
Who've always sought refreshment on their journeys

In times gone by, those church-avoiding sinners
Would have patronised the coaching inns
Along the road to Slough

But now the drive-in trade belongs
To Costa and McDonald's
While the names of former businesses
Are fading from buildings
Like the one near Henlys Roundabout
That used to be a garage –
The Airport Motor Radiator Co...

They'd have done a roaring trade here
With old-timers
In their sports cars and jalopies –
Might have even kept some spares behind the counter
For what Biggles called his kite...

"Look here, old man, we've landed just nearby,
And we need a spot of oil,
Plus a prop lock and a Pitot tube,
A spark plug and perhaps a Very light:
You're saying 'No can do'?
But lots of other flying chums
Have told me about you
And said that you'd be sure to see me right.

"Okay old boy there's no need to get shirty
You're clearly not the feller
I was hoping to do business with today
It was many years ago

So I suppose that he's sold up
Or maybe snuffed it
And since I'm just a ghost myself
You shouldn't pay attention to anything I say..."

There's little space for phantoms
As I close in on the Airport
And no equivocation
On the posted prohibitions –
Beware of special bye-laws, mortal danger
No right of way for crusties
Or for climate-change protestors –
A warning to the curious: keep your distance

And now, above the barriers
An aircraft's tail
Is moving like an animal's
Across the fenced-off spaces

Where giant metal creatures
Rumble as they taxi
Make a revving surging
When they hurtle down the runway

And with it
A massive lengthy fart from the exhaust fumes
A sound and stink that linger in the air
And boom around the highway

As I stood there
I suddenly recalled a dire warning
From a colleague I had lunch with
In the early nineteen-eighties.

"You need to know," she told me,
"That the tin of fizzy drink which you're consuming

Will give you indigestion.
And also: there's a chemical inside it
That'll make you want another and another…"
She was right about the flatulence;
But not the secret formula,
As far as I'm aware.

          Oh, thank you: I don't mind if I do
          But just the one
          At least for now…

For I was half expecting
What happened near the airport:
A product of the sound
    and the excitement and the smell
A sudden wild desire
To find a plane to take me –
As to where, I didn't care –
To Hell with any planning

Was I in the throes
Of something like the craving
That my colleague said I'd suffer
After quaffing down my drink?
Just imagine what the Greens
Would think if it was proven
That the aircraft engine fumes I'd been inhaling
Contained a special substance
(Like the dubious addition to my soda)
Making people want to jump aboard a plane and fly away into the blue
Leaving behind them
A trail of CO_2

MAD FOR IT

(I even shouted out the stupid words:

They were fortunately drowned
In the reverberating noise,
And there was nobody around)

MAD FOR IT

I needed to calm down
And so I headed for a bus stop
But later in the day I went online
To finalise my booking for some flights and a hotel
You'll probably have guessed my destination...

III

MAD FOR IT

Well I think you bloody have to be
To tolerate the levels of security
Before a long-haul flight

I always make an effort
To blend in at the airport –
Try to keep my movements
Smooth and calm and fluent

But as they're frequently disrupted
Could it be
I've got a 'Kick Me' sign that I can't see
Stuck somewhere on my back
Or on my luggage?

"Yes, you there, sir –
Did you know
You haven't got
It's not displaying
Something's triggering our sensor

Step aside here for a moment
You should have filled the form in
Take it off I'm going to grope around
In case there's any contraband
Within those hidden spaces
We apologise for all this inconvenience
False alarm…"

After that I need a coffee
And the pleasant young barista
Smiles and asks me if I'm having a nice day.
She's visibly put out when I reply,
"Well no not really,
But I'll soon be on my way."

It strikes me that our plane
Is merely going through the motions
As it starts its lumbering foreplay
And heads towards the runway.
We're all strapped down
In joyless expectation
Itchy and impatient
Now it pauses on the threshold
                    Get on up
For the moment we'll be
Pinned back in our seats

But take-off is a going not a coming
And already
We can sense the dislocation
In height and in relation to what's passing by below us
Slippery tension
                    like a piece of modern music
                    that combines two separate metres
                    and messes with our heads;
All this is long before our bodies start to notice

The onset of the jet-lag
That's its physical expression

To minimise it,
I set my watch back
And try and get my head around our geodesic pathway
Mapped out in two dimensions
On the tiny screen before me

It tells me San Francisco is five thousand miles away
Ten hours in the air...
Half the time it would have taken
On planes that had prop engines,
Though even that was nothing
Compared to months at sea

And now we're nearly over Liverpool
I think of bygone sailors
Emerging from the port there
And heading south past Holyhead
En route to California round Cape Horn

In October 1850 the *McDonald* sailed from here to San
Francisco via Chile
    On board were
        thirteen iron houses,
        fire bricks and bedsteads,
        mattresses and cisterns,
        and a boiler

Two months later, the cargo of the *Margaret* included
        butter, wine and whiskey,
        iron goods, machines and engines,
        and devices
        to wash the Forty-Niners'
        golden nuggets

There were often passengers as well –
Some listed 'Unidentified in steerage'...

I know even less about the people seated near me
And now the guy beside the window's pulled its shade down
Shutting out the sky and wing
That were the only things in view
I paper over
The looming empty hours and vacant spaces
With thoughts about the progress of a ship called *Lady
Heathcote*
The details of whose passage round the Horn to San Francisco
In 1868 and '69
Were recorded by her carpenter, George Mansfield...

IV

What makes a perfect witness?
John Le Carré says it's someone with no malice
Or personal opinion;
Robert Harris, in *Gotcha!*, suggests that Brian Hanrahan,
Reporting from the Falklands,
Was aided by his ignorance of warfare
And his wonder at the power of its weapons.

George Mansfield knew little of the ocean,
And nothing of the places he'd encounter;
He misspells them in his journal
And gets muddled as to dates when he's at sea.
But he's a watcher, whose words about his voyage
Read like testimony from an honest copper
On the stand, with a notebook in his hand.

*Towed out of dock in Liverpool at seven in the morning
On November the eleventh 1868.
Proceed to sea:
Fresh breeze and foggy weather;*

And next day, when we're passing Bardsey Island,
I watch it dipping in and out the water
As our vessel falls and rises
With the currents that are bearing us away.

Soon the Captain
Has to show his sway and stature:
Two sailors are taken from the wheel,
For they didn't know the compass,
And their steering was improper.

Much later in the voyage
There's trouble with another of my shipmates,
Johnsson the Norwegian.
He's reprimanded by the Captain,
And when others side with Johnsson,
I'm told to grind the cutlasses and get the firearms ready.
Any mutiny's avoided by next morning
When Johnsson sees the Captain
And humbly begs his pardon.

But for now we're heading southwards
Past the island of Madeira;
There'd been a whale beside us
The afternoon before.
And we collided in the darkness
With a brig that had no lights up;
It struck the mizzen rigging, but did no serious damage,
And we had no further sighting of the vessel...

By Christmas Day we're in the South Atlantic,
And are thinking of our loved ones far away.
We know our longing
Cannot bring us back together,
But trust that we will have a happy meeting by and by.
In the meantime, we all enjoy our dinner:
Bouillon, Christmas pudding, and a fine plum cake for tea.

There are even cheese and pickles from the galley –
The last remaining morsels
Of the luxuries and treats we brought to sea.

The changing seasons
Are a confusion:
The weather in December
Is hotter than an English summer's day;
But one month after,
For all that it is now the height of summer
     off Cape Horn,
The cold is more intense
Than any I've encountered –
I don't know what it must be like in winter.

On January the fourteenth 1869
We sight the rugged mountains of Tierra del Fuego:
Its peaks are topped with snow,
Yet here at sea it's warm and fine.

The next day is a Friday: we're becalmed,
And our sails are flapping listlessly...

Ere long the wind is fresh'ning:
If conditions stay the same
We'll soon be up again to the Equator...

We make a splendid run – two hundred miles a day –
But the conclusion of the month is cold and wet,
Depriving us of almost any comfort,
While February commences
With very dirty weather.

We're beginning to get tired of the passage,
And I'm longing for the sight of California.

I feel I'm in the doldrums
At this point in our flight
Though my misusing of the term
Would earn me the disdain of any sailor

For even though the plane has crossed the ocean
And is nearing Hudson Bay
The readout of the mileage is a wearisome reminder
That we're barely come halfway

And though the screen is showing tailwinds
Of a hundred miles an hour
I can't feel them,
And scarcely even register the engines' thrusting power

As to the places we fly over
I conceive them
Just as featureless expanses –
Mere distances to cover...

So I sigh
And pull my blanket closer;
I'll liven up again
Once we've crossed into Montana

    (The carpenter's in better shape than I am,
    Though a couple of his shipmates are ailing...)

Robert Dannely's been suffering from derangement
For nearly two months now;
While another crewman's grievously afflicted with the piles.
But most of us on board the Lady Heathcote
Are now indulging freely
In the hope that we'll be spending
Just two more weeks at sea.
For we're heading through the water
At a splendid rate towards our destination...

On March the twenty-second
I glimpse the Farallon Islands
And in the afternoon the following day
The Pilot comes on board
To guide us into San Francisco Bay.

He'd spent four months at sea,
But Mansfield doesn't tell us what he saw
On reaching *terra firma*,
Or while he was ashore.

He was soon on board the *Heathcote* once again,
For she sailed from San Francisco
On the twenty-fourth of April
And was safely back in England by September.

It won't be long until our own arrival:
We're dazzled by the sunlight in the cabin
As our lethargy gives way
To feelings of community
And pleasant, if sporadic conversation

I think the reason
Is the nearing, warming presence of the City:
We're aren't yet quite in sync
With what's beneath us

But after touch-down, when we stumble
Past vacated rows of seats
Towards the exit door
(The crumpled stuff
They leave behind in Business Class
Is just as stale and nasty
As our garbage in Economy)

We will be

V

"You'd better watch it!" –
The phrase can cover
A range of meanings
From outright threats
To friendly warnings

It's like a turn-up
On the trousers
Of acceptable behaviour
To stop things
Falling downward any further;

You go beyond it
(Or take your pants off)
At your peril

You wouldn't wander naked
Into US Immigration
And you shouldn't accidentally
Tick the boxes on the ESTA form
Confessing you're a spy or saboteur;

I nearly did so, but my error
Was flagged up by the software:
"Is that really what you meant?" –
In other words, "You'd better watch it!"
I was grateful.

"Howdy, stranger!"
There's something sinister
About that greeting –
Words you might expect from guys
In cowboy hats and Western ties,
But not the average Californian.

It draws attention
To my status –
For I know that I'm a stranger,
And recognise that therefore
I'm to some degree a sucker:
An 'innocent abroad' by definition

The sort of person
Who's at risk
Of being taken for a ride;
Who misjudges things,
And fails to read the signs.
At best, a subject
For indulgent toleration –
"Such people don't know any better!" –
At worst, potentially, a victim

So as a sucker and a stranger
I'd be well advised to watch it:
And as I head downtown on BART
My jet-lagged introspection
Begs a question:
"What am I bringing with me?"

Well, flicking through the checklist…
      Nothing that's illegal
      Nothing that's for sale
      Nothing that's infectious

But aside from this, a bundle
Of attitudes and ways
Like stiffened muscles
That need manipulation

I may have had a taste
Of the essence of this place

From books and from TV;
On vinyl and CD and MP3...

But still, the nitty gritty
Of living and transacting here
Is alien to me
For the spirit and the workaday
Are never quite in harmony.

Imagine you're a regular attender at a church:
Accustomed to its liturgy
Familiar with the stands and sits
And tolerant of the cold

But one day you make a visit
To another House of God
Where 'ye' and 'thee' are absent
From the readings and the prayers;
The central heating works;
And Signs of Peace are made
With warm embraces
Instead of sheepish handshakes

Yet whatever the resultant
Shyness and discomfort
Such incompatibilities
Are merely different outer ways
To manifest a message all believers share in essence
So you decide to get in tune with these good people –
Your brothers and your sisters,
Notwithstanding
Their unfamiliarities –
And try to readjust to your surroundings;
But quickly find it's easier said than done:

| Will the choir | Watch the traffic! |
| Turn towards the altar? | It's coming from a different direction |

| How much should you | Does my debit card work here? |
| put in the collection? | I'm not sure what to tip the waiter |

| "I love your accent!" | If you're English in the USA |
| | Steer clear of words like "Ectually" |

| "YOU FUCKING | What's with *this* guy? |
| BASTARD!" | |

Yes: I knew I'd better watch it.
We're at Powell
Where the numbers of the homeless and the desperate
Have grown since the last time I was here.
I'd stopped to sort my tickets out
And straightaway attracted some attention

The ranting man was running round the station
Scarcely begging
Just cursing and demanding

I encountered others like him
On my way along the street
As darkness fell.
Their shouting and their cries
Were like a bitter serenade
Amid the clanging cable cars
And to shut out all the din
Lots of visitors and locals
Had their headphones
Connected to their mobiles

They'd sealed themselves inside a system
That limits interaction
With the people that surround them
And the traffic at the junctions…

I appreciate their reasons –
Even read about a playlist
Of songs that you should listen to
At various locations round the City

And I'm sure the music's fine –
But on my own perambulations
I'd like to hear those places as they are
While, misguidedly, maybe
I want to keep the *solemn stillness*
That (paradoxically) we sing of
In *It Came Upon the Midnight Clear*
At Christmas

Unlike its author, Edmund Sears
    (a Massachusetts pastor),
I've little faith
In *Heav'n's all-gracious King*:
But could it be
That *ever o'er the Babel-sounds* of San Francisco
The blessed angels sing?

VI

All travellers to this City
Must pay homage to the ocean, and the Golden Gate:
Though in doing so
We struggle with the infinite –
    Reach out into parallels and metaphors,
    Or glance across at how our literary betters
        With their finer minds and clearer grasp
        Of scripture and mythology
    Convey the depths and magnitudes
    That lap against our fragile little
    Citadels of certainty

For when the subject is the sea

Their thoughts (and ours) are filled
With archetypal monsters
Whose resonance and names –
Charybdis
          Leviathan
                    and Kraken –
Are always there in our imagination

There are other, gentler beings
In the poems of the ocean –
Like Thomas Shadwell's kindly tritons
Attending voyages
On Purcell's *Halcyon Days* –
But those deep waters
Never lose their dark associations;
Paul Theroux was right about the people
Who gaze in Death's direction
As they sit inside their cars
Along the English shoreline
Staring in silence at the sea

And yet it's all too tempting
To misapply such images;
What might be true in Britain
Or fitting for a Greek or Roman myth
Or in the Bible
May simply not belong in other places:
And if we settle for a cliché
Or the merely picturesque in our descriptions
We can end up stuck in Davy Jones's Locker
Or drowning in the waters of the 'Silv'ry Tay'...

I want to cast aside such formulae today –
Tear them from my mind
And watch them sink
Like tissue paper in the sea

The wind here on the Bridge
Is fierce and leaves me gasping;
Though it also keeps me moving (and my vertigo at bay)

The traffic passing by me
On State Route 1 and US 101
Doesn't linger either
And gives me a reminder
Of what the Bridge is for

While it certainly fulfilled
A grandiose ambition,
      Proclaimed at its inaugural Fiesta in 1937:
      The completion of
      a smooth, unbroken highway
      from Canada to Mexico
It also boosted
The local and commercial...
      The Fiesta had its own
      Official Sandwich;
      while if you fancied something sweeter,
      you could, to quote the ad,
      Say Gear-ar-delly to the Vendor...
And sped up journey times around the region...
      which led to traffic jams
      and helped to put the ferries out of business...

In short, it was and is a *means* –
A structure that for all its high-flown wonder,
Forms a grounded,
Guaranteed support for San Franciscans' undertakings
A unifying presence, not a *yoke* or *overlay* –
And a part of a New World that pays no tribute
To the jealous gods and creatures of other, distant seas.

To my right I see the City, its creator:
A haven and a fortress –
>   *Oro en paz, fierro en guerra*
>   One that has its own Madonna,
>   Identified, I've read,
>   as Santa Niebla,
>   Our Lady of the Fogs:
>   *Ave Maris Stella* –
A place of sweet arrival and provision
And a gateway for departure

Why am I so reluctant
To look out the other way, towards the ocean?
I'm not afraid of Cetus or of Scylla
(Not here in the Pacific);
I don't think even Death is waiting out there in the water.
But maybe there's a Roman myth that's legal tender here:
The one of Janus

Unlike him, though, I'm smiling as I gaze inland;
I can't read my other face, the one that contemplates the
vastness

VII

I thought I'd try to find a pub in Cambridge
Whose exact location I'd forgotten
Though I had a vague idea of its direction
And its distance from the centre of the town

So I pictured little details –
The menu on its blackboard, and the sawdust on its floor –
And tried to use them like a kind of pathway
To guide me through the streets towards its door

I didn't really know where I was going
But after half an hour I'd somehow made it to that bar

Where my beer, and the sandwich from its kitchen
Were just as good as I'd been hoping for

This morning, waking up in San Francisco,
I recalled the smell of croissants, and coffee being roasted
From somewhere in Pacific Heights
I'd been to years before

Could my instinct lead me back towards that café?
Was it even in business any more?
What the hell – the sun was shining, I felt game for anything:
Put my street map in my pocket,
And checked I had a notebook
To write down what I saw

Well, I'd surely earned a snicker from the City's *genius loci*:
And I'd forgotten just how steep the climb would be;
While on my breathless way northwest
Other coffee outlets
Propositioned me...

> *Howdy, stranger!*
> *Take a load off;*
> *Use the rest room:*
> *Why not have a cappuccino*
> *And a complimentary Danish?...*

But instead, I kept right on (like Harry Lauder)
Found a bus to take me up Van Ness,
Then split off to the west...
Where I think my ESP would barely scrape a beta minus,
For I couldn't find the café –
Though I did locate a nearby
Satisfactory place to get my breakfast
And over coffee
I at least arrived at something –

A conclusion:
>Mere intuition doesn't cut it as a means
>To rediscover the locations
>Of former tastes and feelings;

>Its small successes
>Are barely more than serendipity.

>To shift my focus past myself
>And onto what this place can show to me,
>I need to find a better way:
>I'd like to try one out round Kearny, Pacific,
>And the streets towards the Bay

A patriotic question in a physics book at school
Asked us to calculate
How many molecules of Nelson's dying breath
Might still be present in the atmosphere;
Would the figure for the remnants
Of the brothels and the dives
And the theatres and saloons
That once stood here
Be just about as minuscule?

I've seen the pictures;
But fire and changing mores
Have done away with all those places

It's said the barkers and the madams
Didn't like their customers to share too many details
About the goings-on

It's strange to think the status of a house of ill repute
Might depend upon the hookers and the johns
All keeping stumm

But without the spurious lure of secrecy
Initiates shouldn't speak of what they see
or what they've done
I'm not sure there'd have been that many takers

Night-time glimpses
If a window or a door was left ajar
Would only interest a peeping tom or prowler
While in the light of day
We'd see the stains and creases
On the sheets and pillow-cases
In all their ugly clarity

I could be wrong, and anyway,
We're dealing now with history –
Particles and photographs and fragments...

With the curious exception
Of the soundtracks for these spots of dissipation
Whose transitory music
Has left surviving traces

It was mostly nothing more
Than a commodity:
    Sounds to grab attention –
        the blaring gramophones and steam pianos;
    Sounds to have a dance to –
        this punter's overwhelmed by easy pleasure
        when the band begins to play...
        They play such jolly music,
        Waltz, polka and quadrille,
        And sometimes play so feelingly,
        It gives me quite a thrill...;
    Songs to sing along to –
        the words appeared on broadsides
        published in their thousands
        by companies like Boyd's

at Montgomery and Pine.
They can't be read today without a shudder,
though the ghastly-titled *Pretty Octoroon –*
Dressed in the highth of fashion,
with *a darling roguish eye –*
would draw *immense applause*
for a minstrelsy performer called Joe Murphy,
who sang and played the bones
at a music hall nearby

Other local venues
Hosted more distinguished artists:
Pianist Sid LeProtti; and even (on Columbus)
Mr Jelly Roll himself, from New Orleans...
But did their customers esteem those finer sounds?
Were they *aficionados*?
Or was the music just a background
For a card game, some dancing, and whatever else went
down?

I'd like to think that the musicians
Knew their compositions
Could never be confined
Within those seedy spaces

The other stuff, however,
Found its fate among the rubble and the ashes,
Although it still emits some faint vibrations:
  Remember me?
Well, no –
And all I've done today
Is try to listen for your echo:
But now it's time to go.

VIII

Some cities
Present us
With immaculate façades
Some are diamonds in the rough
A few are turds

But San Francisco's gleam and glow
Can be tracked throughout the day;
I begin at Old St Mary's –
Whose clock displays a warning
To sojourners like me:
    Son, observe the time, and fly from evil.

Am I guilty, this morning, of
The deadly sin of sloth
By standing here and taking in
The cascading silver sheen
From sunlight on
Deliveries of fish in Chinatown?

Well, Ecclesiastes says that
Truly, the light's a sweet and pleasant thing to see –
So I give myself a pass, and climb higher up Nob Hill
To catch the rays of afternoon
On the buildings and the ocean
While at close of day
    Now we are come to the sun's hour of rest;
My chosen vantage point
    The lights of evening round us shine;
Is Pioneer Park
    We hymn the Father,
Where what I see –
    Son,
although I don't ascribe
    and Holy Spirit

the wonder of the scene
to any deity –
            divine!
Somehow
Comes across more finely
In those verses by John Keble
(Translated from the Greek:
            Phôs hilaròn –
            Hail! gladdening Light)
Even though he never came here
Than by any words of mine

A city's partially defined
By the attitude it strikes
As its suburbs
Encroach
On vacant space and wilderness

The roads
        gain traffic lights and intersections;
And there are signs
        for local destinations
Instead of less specific indications
        (*West* and *South,* or merely highway numbers)

I was weary
On a journey down the seaboard
I'd taken with a colleague
Some fifteen years ago

The 4x4 we'd hired
Was much the worse for wear
And our hollow-eyed demeanour
Must have showed;

For when we stopped to get some gas outside the City,
A passer-by came over
To ask us, rather warily,
"You guys – how long have you been on the road?"

We were pleased to see a friendly face
After previous encounters with some cops
 (*You fellas ran that light! Are you from Ireland?*),
And a threatening pair of hunters
Who'd driven close behind us
Through the forests up the coast

I'd had enough of backwoods
(And of trees, I have to say):
I was eager to return to urban life,
And for somewhere on a city street to stay

But first, we had to make it into town
And get ourselves off Highway 101
Which, it seemed to me,
Didn't want us to break free

Was there a False Knight on this Road
Like in the ballad?
A trickster or a demon
Whose questions must be parried
With suitable replies?
How might our conversation with him be?

  What brings you here so late?
  How will you go by land?
  How will you go by sea?
Well, there's a bridge
To span the waters of the Bay;
We'll stay in lane,
Obey the signs;

And it isn't very late –
Not even lighting-up time yet...
                    You must be Brits to talk like that!
                    So tell me – what you got in back?
Our bundles and our books...
                    OK, but what's that in your hand?
It's nothing but a map:
We're looking for an exit...
                    Ha ha! Got you there! Wrong way!
But we didn't make a turn,
And there are ten more miles to go...
                    That's what you reckon?
                    Your map is out of date: c'mon!
                    You guys don't even know
                    Which way you're headed.
                    Hey, I think I hear a bell!
Yes, it's ringing you to Hell!
                    Oh shit: I guess you know the song!
                    So now I'll have to let you go;
                    I could recommend a cheap motel...
That's kind of you, but no.

For as we closed in on the City
The roads beyond the off-ramps
Were like ribbons
From a trailing silken garment
Lying softly by the highway;
And the place names on the signs
Were sonorous enticements –
Mill Valley, Sausalito...
Then something more prosaic:
Exit 437 –
Presidio/Marina Boulevard
The route off 101
Towards our bed and breakfast in Cow Hollow...

IX

On that trip
I was able to check out the *Little Boxes*
That Malvina Reynolds scoffed at in her song;
They're on the slopes of Daly City
And I found their vivid colours
Undeserving of her scorn

Her number surely served its purpose
As a tool in the progressives'
Endless struggle, and a big hit for Pete Seeger...
But time passes, targets shift, and I dare say
If Malvina still were with us,
She'd be fighting on a different front today

And I see she had a Masters and a doctorate from Berkeley –
Whose other students have included Dr Leary (LSD),
Steve Wozniak of Apple,
Jack London,
Susan Sontag;
None of them conformists
Like the stereotypes she sang of:
But anyway...

Her *alma mater's* peaceful
On this sunny afternoon
There's a feeling of transition
As I take the short walk east from Berkeley station
To the campus

Do the air-vents from its buildings
Exude the scent of Scholarship and Protest?
Confrontation and Free Speech?
No, it's just the eucalyptus.
And despite our easy access to the paths and open spaces
Security is strict

And though we're welcome in the cafés and the pizza joints
and bookshops,
Other doors are closed politely in our faces.

To any stranger's knowledge of this City (and this country)
There are limits:
We'll never see material stamped with NOFORN
        (Spook-speak: *not for eyes of foreign nationals*) –
While in daily interactions
We stand apart like pebbles
Left unshaped and dry by tides
That residents are always in the swim of
        (I'm sure we'd be more skilful
        At hiding in plain sight
        If we were really spies)

And we cling to our distortions and illusions
Like children to their teddies –
To words from other visitors
That may have little resonance for native San Franciscans:
Stevenson's description of
        "indefinite prolongation of its streets"…
And Oscar Wilde's assertion –
        "anyone who disappears" is said to be seen here…

I know it's an imperfect simile,
But the City's lofty stacks of buildings
Seem to me like shelving in a library;
A place where almost anyone
Can occupy a niche and gain a label:

In 1921, Almira Bailey wrote of
Old American stock,
Lumberjacks, philosophers,
Mexicans, Sinn Feiners,

Chinamen in slippers,
Turbaned Hindus, Portuguese
and many others at the Port.
Thankfully, diversity today
Is flagged up more respectfully;
For San Francisco needs its passers-through,
And immigrants
And strangers

Since gold-rush days
There's been an urgency and longing to arrive here:
In a story by Samuel Adams Drake
1850s vessels
Berthed in Boston Harbour
Carried signs upon their rigging
Declaring they were headed *with dispatch for San Francisco*

But now, as a result of the contagion
That's gripping California and the nation,
We've seen the digital displays
Of airline cancellations
And the plight of passengers in Oakland
Aboard the *Grand Princess*
Who had the virus...

Nothing fundamental in the elements has changed.
Tides and jet-streams haven't lost their power
To bring us in on ships and planes:
But till it's safe to come and go,
Would-be visitors
Can only wait at home
For favourable conditions.

And at a time when facile comments
And half-truths and evasions
Are two a penny from our politicians,

Outsiders ought to weigh their words with care

I'm well aware my own uncertainties
Regarding my return
Have no significance to anyone but me;
But I look forward to the day
When I hear the City ask me in again
With a whisper on the breeze across the Bay

GOING NOWHERE
Exploring London's Abandoned Places

Text by Nick Freeth, photos by Olivia Landsberg

Going Nowhere is about places that have become disconnected from modern London: discarded parts of the capital's infrastructure; once-crucial facilities that it's outgrown; remnants of bold schemes that never quite came about.

It tells the stories of these desolate sites. It examines their history and context, explains why they were created, and discovers what admirers and denigrators had to say about them. It also considers them more subjectively, seeking to convey their enduring ambience and character, and even uncover some of their ghosts.

'If you wondered how come London is full of stubs, dead ends and unfinished business, this book will explain how and why. A lovely take on our great city with lots of interesting stories and lots of answers for pub quizzers.'
Christian Wolmar, author of *The Subterranean Railway*, the story of the London Underground

Published by Baffin Books, price £9.99